Tex-Mex

100 Recipes to Spice Up Your Appetite

Tera L. Davis

TERA L. DAVIS

Copyright © 2012 Tera L. Davis
All rights reserved.

ISBN-13: 978-1480172999

100 Recipes to Spice Up Your Appetite _____ *1*
Homemade Tortilla Chips _____ 10
Taco Shells _____ 11
Enchiladas _____ *12*
Beef _____ *12*
Creamy Enchiladas _____ 12
So Saucy Enchiladas _____ 14
Cheesy Beef Enchiladas _____ 15
Enchilada Stack _____ 16
Chicken _____ *17*
Green Chili Enchiladas _____ 17
So Easy Crockpot Enchiladas _____ 18
Spicy Chicken Enchiladas _____ 19
Green Chilies & Chicken Enchiladas _____ 20
Mozzarella Chicken Enchiladas _____ 21
Vegetable _____ *22*
Flat Spinach Enchiladas _____ 22
Rolled Spinach Enchiladas _____ 24
Casseroles _____ *25*
Beef _____ *25*
Tortilla Chip Casserole _____ 25
Taco Casserole _____ 26
Yummy Enchilada Casserole _____ 27
Hardy Mexican Casserole _____ 28
Fast & Easy Enchilada Casserole _____ 29

Mexican Casserole	30
Tortilla Casserole	31
Tasty Taco Casserole	32
Enchilada Casserole	33
Mexican Casserole	34
Chicken	*35*
Tex Mex Chicken Casserole	35
Green Chili Chicken Casserole	36
Chili Chicken Casserole	37
Tacos	*38*
Easy Meat & Potato Tacos	38
Soft Chicken Tacos	39
Taco Snacks	40
Taco Appetizer	41
Quesadillas	*42*
Beef Quesadillas	42
Chicken Quesadillas	43
Veggie Quesadillas	44
So Easy Quesadillas	45
Green Chili Quesadillas	46
Chili Rellenos	*47*
Chili Rellenos	47
Chili Relleno Bake	48
Burritos	*49*
Beef Burritos	49
Breakfast Burritos	50
Turkey Bacon Burrito	51

Roxitos Burritos ... 52

Mexican Meat Pies ... 54

Frito Pie ... 54
Tamale Pie ... 55
Oven Baked Frito Pie ... 56
Tasty Taco Pie ... 57
Nacho Pie ... 58
Impossible Taco Pie ... 59
Tamale Pie ... 60

Fajitas ... 61

Sizzling Fajitas ... 61
Chicken Fajita Potatoes ... 62

More Tex-Mex Meat Dishes ... 63

Mexican Pile On with Pecans & Coconut ... 63
Peccadillo ... 64
Tex-Mex Chicken Stew ... 65
Tex-Mex Pork Chops ... 66
Tortilla Pinwheels ... 67
Tex-Mex Lasagna ... 68
Mexican Hot Dish ... 69
Mexican Chicken ... 70

Salads ... 71

Texas Taco Salad ... 71
Cheesy Taco Salad ... 72
Mexican Corn Relish Salad ... 73
Taco Salad ... 74
Taco Frito Salad ... 75

Mexican Salad	76
Steak Taco Salad	77
Delicious Taco Salad	78

Soups — 79

Mexican Cheese Soup	79
Texas Taco Soup	80
Stewed Taco Soup	81
Mexican Meatball Soup	82

Salsas — 83

Zesty Salsa	83
Salsa	84

Dips — 85

Seven Layer Dip	85
Fiesta Dip	86
Easy Chili Dip	87
Mexican Dip	88
Easy Nacho Cheese Dip	89
Hardy Tex-Mex Dip	90
Chili Cheese Dip	91
Cheesy Taco Dip	92
Hot Taco Cheese Dip	93
Mexican Dip	94
Texas Caviar	95
Easy Taco Dip	96
Party Taco Dip	97
Mexican Meat Dip	98
Baked Nacho Dip	99

Chili Dip	100
Layered Taco Dip	101
Nacho Cheese Dip	102
Nacho Dip	103
Mexican Dip	104
Jalapeno Corn Dip	105
Guacamole	*106*
Tasty Guacamole Dip	106
Holy Guacamole	107
Breads	*108*
Texas Cornbread	108
Mexican Cornbread	109
Desserts	*110*
Cinnamon Apple Enchiladas	110
Sweet Banana Bake	111
Mexican Fiesta Pie	112
Miscellaneous	*113*
Baked Jalapeno Poppers	113
Mexican Quick Steppers	114
My Mexican Deviled Eggs	115

Tex-Mex Recipes

Authentic Mexican Food

Mexican food has an interesting and diverse history. This American favorite is believed to have started with the Mayan Indians. The Mayan's had a diet rich in fish, tropical fruit and wild game; but they also were known to make and eat corn tortillas with beans that were cooked and turned into paste and placed upon the tortilla. Could this of been the first soft taco?

When Spain invaded Mexico in 1521, the Spanish cuisine came along with them. The Spanish brought new foods and animals to Mexico such as cows, sheep and pigs. Garlic, dairy products, wheat, spices and certain herbs were also introduced. In certain regions of Mexico tortillas were being made along with meat being cooked and place along with beans onto the tortilla, not to mention all the herbs and spices added for flavor. Mexicans found an inexpensive and simple meal for their families that was delicious and nutritious.

Tex-Mex Arrives

The word Tex-Mex originated as a nickname for the Texas/Mexico railway in the year of 1875.

We do things in a BIG way here in the Lone Star state and Tex-Mex food is no exception! Mexican food started making its way across the Texas-Mexico border and Texans started adding to the already delicious cuisine. Texans living in south Texas started adding more beef, spices and introducing cheese to top off these wonderful dishes. Without the invention of Tex-Mex we wouldn't have such food items as crispy tacos, chili gravy, crispy chalupas, chili con queso, fajitas, casseroles and chili con carne.

It's rare to find a meal that is absolutely delicious, filling and pleasing to the eye and palate that is relatively inexpensive and so easy to create. Here you will find a variety of Tex-Mex recipes that will please your families and friends and have them leaving the dinner table with a full belly and a smile on their faces.

Enjoy browsing through these wonderful recipes and start serving up Tex-Mex in your kitchen.

Did you know you can make your own tortilla chips and taco shells? Read how with these easy to follow recipes below:

Homemade Tortilla Chips

1 package corn tortillas (12 ct.)
Cooking oil
Salt

With a sharp knife cut tortillas into triangle shaped wedges, you should yield 4 to 6 wedges per tortilla.

Pour cooking oil into a deep fryer or use 3/4 cup of oil into a deep sided frying pan. When using a deep fryer be sure to read & follow the manufacturer's instructions.

When frying chips in a frying pan; heat cooking oil for approximately one (1) minute. Drop a small piece of a tortilla into the oil and if it sinks to the bottom, oil is not hot enough yet. When tortilla bubbles up and floats on top of oil... it's ready to go!

Using a spatula or metal spoon with drainage holes, slide a few tortilla pieces into oil. Fry until crispy & golden brown in color, should take less than 1 minute. Drain chips on top of paper towels and sprinkle with sea salt or regular table salt. Enjoy!

Taco Shells

1 pkg. corn tortillas
Cooking oil

Pour cooking oil into pan and heat over medium heat. Fold tortilla into a shape of a taco shell and using tongs fry each side in hot oil until light brown and crispy.
Stand open side of shell onto a paper towel until it is set. Repeat this method and place each cooked taco shell one on top of the other. Only place a cooked taco shell on top of a taco shell that is already set.

Once all the taco shells are set, fill with your favorite taco foods.

Enchiladas

Beef

Creamy Enchiladas

1 ½ lb. of hamburger
1 can cream of mushroom soup
1 can of mild enchilada sauce
1 small can of chopped green chilies (optional)
2 cups of shredded cheddar cheese
1 pkg. of corn tortillas (20 ct)
½ cup of cooking oil

Preheat oven to 350 degrees F

In a skillet, fry hamburger meat (salt & pepper to taste) until fully cooked; drain and set aside. In a sauce pan, combine soup, enchilada sauce and green chilies, heat on low, stirring occasionally. While your sauce simmers, heat cooking oil in skillet till hot, place one tortilla at a time into oil, turning quickly then remove immediately and start another one. (Tortillas should be placed 4 at a time between paper towels to help absorb the oil).

Once you have cooked all the tortillas, take a 9 X 13 inch baking pan and coat the bottom and edges of the pan with ¼ cup of the enchilada sauce or with cooking spray. Place 2 to 3 tablespoons of hamburger meat into one tortilla then roll. Place rolled & meat filled tortillas side by side with the folded edge down.

Pour the enchilada sauce over the rolled enchiladas and then top with the shredded cheddar cheese. Cover pan with aluminum foil, place in preheated oven and cook until cheese is melted and sauce is bubbly, approximately 30 to 45 minutes.

So Saucy Enchiladas

1 (8 oz.) can tomato sauce
1 ½ cups water
1 lb. ground beef or ground turkey
8 lg. corn or floured tortillas
2 cups shredded cheddar cheese
1 pkg. enchilada sauce mix (McCormick)

Preheat oven 350 degrees F

In saucepan, combine sauce mix, tomato sauce, and water. Bring to a boil; simmer 5 minutes. Set aside. Brown beef or turkey; drain fat. Stir ½ cup sauce into meat.
Coat tortillas with sauce. Place 3 tablespoons of the meat mixture on each tortilla. Roll meat filled tortillas and place with seam-side down onto a 12 x 7 inch baking dish. Pour remaining sauce over enchiladas. Sprinkle cheese on top and bake for 15 to 20 minutes.

Cheesy Beef Enchiladas

1 lb. ground beef
1 (16 oz.) jar salsa
2 cups sharp cheddar cheese, grated
10 flour or corn tortillas

Preheat oven 350 degrees F

Brown the meat in a skillet and drain, mix in ½ cup salsa & 1 cup of cheese. Place 1 cup of salsa in 9 x 13 inch baking dish and spread across the bottom. On each tortilla place 3 tablespoons of the meat mixture. Roll up. Place rolled tortilla seam-side down on top of salsa. Top with remaining ½ cup salsa and 1 cup cheese. Bake 20 to 25 minutes.

Enchilada Stack

1 lb. lean ground beef or turkey
2 teaspoons olive oil
1 cup chopped onion
1 cup chopped green pepper
1 cup salsa
1½ teaspoons cumin
1½ teaspoons chili powder
6-6 inch tortillas
1 cup nonfat sour cream
4 oz. low fat jack cheese, grated
1 cup cooked corn, drained

Brown meat, oil, onion and green pepper; drain. Add Salsa, cumin, chili powder and simmer 5 minutes. Spray a 9 inch pie pan and layer 2 tortillas, then top that off with a portion of the meat mixture, sour cream and cheese. Repeat to make 3 layers. Top with corn. Cover loosely with foil. Bake 40 minutes at 350 degrees F. Let stand 10 minutes before serving. Makes 8 servings.

Chicken

Green Chili Enchiladas

2 large cans white meat chicken (drained)
(or a roasted chicken)
1 can green chili enchilada sauce
1 can cream of chicken soup
1 pkg. (20 ct.) white corn tortillas
2 cups of shredded Colby Jack cheese

Preheat oven 350 degrees F

Spray non-stick cooking spray onto a 9 X 13 pan. In a large bowl, mix soup and enchilada sauce. Place canned or roasted chicken onto a plate and shred with a fork. Heat tortillas (10 at a time) in the microwave for 30 seconds to make them soft and pliable. Place 2 to 3 tablespoons of chicken onto tortilla, roll and place seam side down into pan, place enchiladas side by side. Cover enchiladas with sauce and top with cheese. Cover pan with aluminum foil and cook for 30 to 45 minutes.

So Easy Crockpot Enchiladas

3 chicken breasts (boneless & skinless)
1 large can green enchilada sauce
1 pkg. flour tortillas
1 to 2 cups shredded Colby jack cheese

Place entire can of enchilada sauce and chicken breast into a crock pot. On low heat, cook all day, until chicken is completely done. Remove chicken from crock pot, shred chicken and place back into crock pot.

Place a heated tortilla onto a dinner plate and spoon a couple of tablespoons of the chicken, sauce and cheese onto it. Roll the tortilla up and place seam down onto the plate, pour a portion of the sauce mixture over the rolled tortilla and heat in microwave for approximately 20 seconds until cheese and sauce are hot and bubbly.

Top with sour cream if desired.

Spicy Chicken Enchiladas

3 cooked boneless chicken breast (shredded)
2 cans tomato sauce (8 oz cans)
1 cup water
2 tablespoons chili powder
½ cup yellow onion (diced)
12 white corn tortillas
3 cups grated cheddar cheese

Preheat oven 400 degree F

Spray a 13 x 9 inch pan with cooking spray and set aside.

In a medium sized saucepan combine 1 cup water, chili powder and tomato sauce. Heat mixture over medium heat until boiling. Reduce heat and simmer for 10 minutes, stirring occasionally. In a large non-stick skillet mix together chicken, onion and a tablespoon of water & cook over medium-high heat 3 to 4 minutes, stirring occasionally.

Using a damp paper towel wrap the tortillas and microwave for one (1) minute. Place 2 to 3 tablespoons of chicken onto tortilla, sprinkle with cheese, roll and place in baking dish seam side down. Pour tomato sauce mixture on top of the rolled enchiladas and top with cheese. Cover pan with aluminum foil.

Bake for approximately 30 minutes.

Green Chilies & Chicken Enchiladas

2 large grilled or baked chicken breast (shredded or cubed)
8 oz. sour cream
1/3 cup diced onion
1 small can diced black olives
1 small can diced green chilies
1 can cream of chicken soup
12 white corn tortillas
2 cups pepper jack cheese (shredded)

Preheat oven to 350 degrees F

In a mixing bowl, mix sour cream, onion, black olives, green chilies, soup and cheese. Divide mixture in half.

Spray a 9 x 13 inch pan with cooking spray.

In the first half of the mixtures add the chicken. Place 2 tablespoons of this mixture onto a single tortilla, roll up and place seam side down onto a cooking pan, do the same on all the tortillas or until pan is full.

Pour the remaining mixture on top of the rolled tortillas, sprinkle with cheese. Cover pan with foil and cook for 35 minutes or until hot and bubbly.

Mozzarella Chicken Enchiladas

4 large skinless & boneless chicken breast (cooked & shredded)
1 bunch of green onions (chopped)
4 cups of shredded mozzarella cheese
2 cans of cream of chicken soup
2 cups of sour cream
2 cans of diced green chili peppers
Salt & pepper to taste
10 flour tortillas
Chicken broth

Preheat oven to 350 degrees F

Mix together chicken, green onions and approximately 1/3 of the cheese and set aside. In a separate bowl, mix soup, sour cream, green chili peppers and salt & pepper; add chicken broth until mixture has a soup consistency.
Spread a portion of the soup mixture onto the bottom of a 9 x 13 inch pan. Place 2 tablespoons of the chicken mixture onto each tortilla roll and place seam down on the pan. Cover with the remainder of the soup mixture and top with shredded cheese.

Bake covered for 30 to 45 minutes.

Vegetable

Flat Spinach Enchiladas

1 ½ cups Colby jack cheese (shredded)
1 pkg. (10 oz) frozen spinach (thawed & drained)
1 pkg. white corn tortillas (20 ct.)
1 yellow onion (diced)
1 small can black olives (chopped)
1 can green enchilada sauce (20 oz)
2 cups sour cream

Preheat oven 350 degrees F

Mix sour cream, thawed spinach and half of shredded cheese in a mixing bowl. Lightly grease a 9 x 13 cooking dish, or spray with cooking spray.

Place 6 of the white corn tortillas on to the bottom of the baking dish. Spoon half of the sour cream mixture, half the yellow onion and half the black olives on top of the tortillas and spread out evenly and repeat.

Once the 2 layers are completed, pour the green enchilada sauce over the layers.

Place the remaining chopped black olives on top.

Bake for 20 minutes or until hot.

Rolled Spinach Enchiladas

5 oz of sour cream
1 can cream of chicken soup
5 oz of frozen spinach (thawed & drained)
1/2 cups pepper jack cheese (shredded)
1/2 cups cheddar cheese (shredded)
6 white corn tortillas

Preheat over 325 degrees F

Fry tortillas in hot oil in skillet (drain on paper towels) or warm in microwave for 1 minute. Place soup, 3/4 of the sour cream and all the spinach into a food processor or blender and blend together. Place 2 tablespoons of the spinach mixture onto a single tortilla, sprinkle with cheese (both cheddar & pepper jack) and roll up, place onto a cooking pan seam down.
Combine the remaining sour cream to the spinach mixture and pour over rolled tortillas.

Bake 15 to 20 minutes.

Casseroles

Beef

Tortilla Chip Casserole

2 lbs. ground beef
1 can cream of chicken soup
1 can cream of mushroom soup
1 bag of Mexican cheese (shredded)
1 can Rotel® tomatoes
½ chopped purple onion (optional)

Preheat oven 350 degree F

Crumble ground beef into a skillet and brown (drain off excess fat). In a large bowl combine Rotel®, soups, corn and chopped onion. Spray non-stick spray on to a large casserole dish; spread half a bag of tortilla chips across the bottom. Place ground beef into the mixture, pour over the tortillas chips. Sprinkle the bag of shredded cheese on top. Bake 30 – 45 minutes.

Taco Casserole

1 ½ pounds of ground beef
1 pkg. taco seasoning
2 cups Colby jack (shredded)
2 cups chunky salsa (mild)
2 green onions (diced)
1 large tomato (diced)
1 small can black olives (sliced)
2 cups corn chips (crushed)
1 can refried beans

Preheat oven 350 degrees F

Crumble ground beef into large non-stick skillet (salt & pepper to taste) cook until well done, drain, add packaged taco seasoning and cook according directions. Starting with refried beans & meat, make 2 layers of the above ingredients in a 9 x 13 inch baking dish.

Bake until hot and bubbly.

Yummy Enchilada Casserole

1.5 lbs. ground beef
1 cup medium yellow onion (chopped)
1 teaspoon minced garlic
1 ½ teaspoons cumin
2 teaspoons chili powder
1 ½ teaspoon salt
½ teaspoon black pepper
1 cup water
2 cups taco sauce
12 corn tortillas
1 cup sour cream
2 cups Monterrey Jack cheese (shredded)

Preheat oven 350 degrees F

In a non-stick skillet brown ground beef, onions and garlic, then drain. Add seasonings and water to the ground beef mix well and simmer uncovered. Spread half of the taco sauce onto the bottom of a 9 x 13 inch cooking pan. Layer half of the tortillas, half the taco sauce, half the ground beef, half sour cream and half the shredded cheese. You will end up with 2 layers.

Cover pan with foil and bake for 40 minutes. Bake an additional 5 minutes uncovered.

Serve with salad, Mexican rice, additional taco sauce and sour cream.

Hardy Mexican Casserole

3 cups zucchini (chopped)
3 Tablespoon margarine or butter
1.5 lbs. ground beef
6 to 8 whole tomatoes (diced)
1 green bell pepper (sliced in strips)
Salt & pepper (to taste)
Chili powder (to taste)
4 Tablespoon taco sauce
1 pkg. tortilla chips
1 ½ cups Colby cheese (shredded)

Preheat oven 350 degrees F

Brown chopped zucchini in margarine and set aside. Brown ground beef and drain. Place zucchini, tomatoes, green pepper and seasonings into ground beef and mix well.

Empty meat mixture into a casserole dish and bake covered for 1 hour. Stir in tortilla chips, top with cheese and bake for an additional 5 minutes uncovered.

Fast & Easy Enchilada Casserole

1 lb. ground beef
1 cup cottage cheese
1 cup sour cream
2 cans of enchilada sauce (hot or mild)
1 pkg. of large flour tortillas

Preheat oven 350 degrees F

Brown ground beef and drain, add cottage cheese, sour cream and 1 can of enchilada sauce, mix well

Turn off heat and place 3 tablespoons of meat mixture onto a flour tortilla, roll up and place seam down onto a greased 9 x 13 inch baking pan.

Once you have rolled your tortillas, pour the other can of enchilada sauce over them.

Bake covered for 20 minutes.

Mexican Casserole

Tortilla chips (bite-size)
2 lbs. ground beef
1 ½ pkg. taco seasoning
Chopped green pepper
Chopped onion
1 lg. jar taco sauce, real chunky
1 (16 oz.) ricotta cheese mixed with 1 ½ cup sour cream
2 lb. pkg. Mexican shredded cheese (4 cheese mixture)

Preheat oven 350 degrees F

Grease 9 x 13-inch casserole dish and layer crushed tortilla chips, cooked ground beef mixed with taco seasoning (drained), chopped green pepper, chopped onion, Ricotta cheese, and sour cream mixture. Pour bottle of taco sauce over casserole. Top with cheese. Bake 45 minutes to 1 hour.

Tortilla Casserole

1 ½ lbs ground chuck
2 Tablespoons salad oil
1 onion, chopped
1 stalk celery, chopped
1 green pepper, chopped
1 cup rice
1 (15 oz.) can red kidney beans, drained
1 cup sliced olives, black or green
1 (28 oz.) can diced tomatoes
1 cup water
2 teaspoons salt
2 Tablespoons chili powder
¼ teaspoon black pepper
1 Tablespoon Worcestershire sauce

Preheat oven 350 degrees F

Brown ground chuck in a skillet. Drain. Transfer to a large casserole dish. In the same skillet, heat salad oil and sauté onion, celery, green pepper and raw rice for a few minutes until rice begins to lightly brown and vegetables soften. Add this mixture to casserole containing the ground chuck. Pour kidney beans, olives, diced tomatoes, water, salt, chili powder, pepper and Worcestershire sauce over the meat, vegetable and rice mixture. Mix well. Top with shredded cheese. Bake covered for approximately 45 minutes to 1 hour.

Tasty Taco Casserole

1 lb. ground beef
1 can refried beans
1 pkg. taco seasoning
1 (8 oz.) pkg. grated cheddar cheese
1 cup milk
1 ½ cup Bisquick mix
2 eggs
1 (8 oz.) sour cream
2 cups shredded lettuce
1 med. diced tomato
1 (2 ¼ oz.) can sliced ripe olives, drained

Preheat oven 400 degrees F

Cook beef and drain, stir in the beans and taco seasoning mix. Spoon onto a greased 8-inch square baking pan and sprinkle cheddar cheese on top. Combine milk, eggs and Bisquick. Mix until moistened and pour evenly over cheese. Bake uncovered for 20 to 25 minutes or until lightly browned and an inserted knife comes out clean. Top with sour cream, lettuce, tomato and olives.

Enchilada Casserole

1 lb. ground beef
1 lb. Longhorn cheddar cheese
1 large onion
1 large green pepper
2 doz. Tortillas
1 container taco sauce
2 cans tomato sauce (with mushrooms or onions or plain)
Canola oil

Preheat oven 350 degree F

Step 1: Grate cheese. Chop onions and green pepper. Step 2: Brown meat with green pepper, drain & set aside. Step 3: Combine taco sauce and tomato sauce and heat slightly. Step 4: Heat tortillas by turning quickly in skillet of hot oil, drain tortillas on paper towels. Dip into sauce mixture and begin layering in bottom of rectangular pan. Step 5: Continuing layering ground meat, cheese, onions, tortillas, etc., until all ingredients are gone. Pour excess sauce over top of casserole. Heat in oven until all ingredients are warmed throughout (30 to 45 minutes). Serve with tortilla chips. Serves 10 to 12.

Mexican Casserole

2 lbs. ground beef
1 jar chunky salsa
1 1/2 cups sour cream
2 cans chopped black olives (small)
1 bag tortilla chips
1 cup cheddar cheese (shredded)

Preheat oven 350 degrees F

Brown ground beef in skillet and drain off fat. Mix meat and salsa together and place in baking pan, heat in over for ½ hour. Take out and layer sour cream on top. Top with chopped black olives. Crush about ½-bag of tortilla chips on top. Top with shredded cheddar and return to oven long enough to melt cheese. Place whole chips around edges and serve.

Chicken

Tex Mex Chicken Casserole

2 large cans white chicken (drained)
1 bag tortilla chips
2 cups cheddar cheese (grated)
¼ cup yellow onion (chopped)
¼ cup bell pepper (chopped)
½ teaspoon garlic powder
1 can cream of mushroom soup
1 can tomatoes with green chilies (10 oz)
2 cans cream of chicken soup

Preheat oven 350 degree F

Spread out tortilla chips onto a 9 x 13 pan. Place chicken on top of chips. Mix together the soups, tomatoes with green chilies, garlic, onion and green bell peppers and pour over the top of chicken. Sprinkle grated cheese on top. Bake for 1 hour.

Green Chili Chicken Casserole

1 yellow onion (chopped)
1 cup chicken broth
2 tablespoons butter
1 can cream of mushroom soup
1 can chopped green chilies (small)
1 can cream of chicken soup
2 lbs. cooked chicken (shredded or cubed)
1 pkg. white corn tortillas
2 cups pepper jack cheese (shredded)

Preheat oven 350 degree F

In a heated skillet brown onion in butter. Combine cooked onion with soups, broth, green chilies and chicken (mix well).

In a greased 9 x 13 inch pan make 2 layers of corn tortillas, chicken mixture and cheese.

Bake for 1 hour.

Chili Chicken Casserole

Bag of tortilla chips
2 15 oz. cans of chili (no beans)
2 chicken breasts
4 cups cheddar cheese (shredded)
2 tablespoons diced jalapeno peppers

Preheat oven 350 degrees F

Boil chicken breast for 20 minutes or until done. Remove skin and shred meat. Mix chili with 1 can of water in a medium sized bowl.

Place a layer of tortilla chips on the bottom of a 2 quart casserole dish. Then layer with half the chili, half the chicken, half the shredded cheese and half the jalapeno peppers.

Repeat layers and top with a layer of tortilla chips.

Cover and cook for 25 minutes, then uncover and cook for 5 minutes.

Tacos

Easy Meat & Potato Tacos

1 lb. ground beef
2 large peeled potatoes (diced-bite size)
1 chopped onion
2 minced garlic cloves
8 ounces tomato sauce
Salt & pepper
12-16 corn tortillas
Cooking oil

Brown ground beef, onion and garlic till well done, then drain (salt & pepper to taste). Boil the diced potatoes until tender. In a large bowl combine ground beef mixture, potatoes and tomato sauce. Warm the tortillas then stack them in a bowl to stay warm. Place a large spoon full of mixture onto the center of the tortilla, wrap and close with a toothpick. Fry in hot oil until crispy.

Soft Chicken Tacos

1 pkg. taco seasoning
3 skinless & boneless chicken breast (shredded)
8 small soft or crispy corn tortillas
1/3 cup yellow onion (chopped)
3 tablespoons butter
½ cup bell pepper (chopped)
1 cup cheddar cheese (shredded)
1 cup lettuce (shredded)
Chunky salsa

Using a large resealable plastic bag place taco seasoning and a portion of the chicken at a time then seal and shake until chicken is well coated.
Cook chicken in 2 tablespoons of butter in a large non-stick skillet for approximately 5 minutes or until well done. Place cooked chicken into a large bowl and keep it warm.
In the same skillet, sauté bell pepper and yellow onion in the remaining butter for 2 to 3 minutes, then stir in chicken. Wrap tortillas in a damp paper towel and heat in the microwave for 1 minute. Spoon mixture onto warmed tortillas and top with cheese, lettuce and salsa.

Taco Snacks

1 stick of butter
9 oz. can of shoestring potatoes
1 pound peanuts
2 cans fried onion rings
1 pkg. Shilling's mild taco seasoning mix

Melt butter in a 9 x 13 inch pan at 250 degrees. Mix shoestring potatoes, peanuts and onion rings with the butter to coat. Sprinkle taco seasoning mix over all, mixing well. Bake at 250 degrees for 45 minutes, stirring every 15 minutes. Store tightly covered.

Taco Appetizer

1 (8 oz.) cream cheese
Lemon juice to taste
Garlic salt to taste
Milk to taste
1 lb. hamburger
1 pkg. taco seasoning
1 onion (chopped)
Tomatoes
1 can sliced black olives (large)
1 cup cheddar cheese (grated)
1 jar taco sauce

Mix first four ingredients together. Cook hamburger and taco seasoning mix according to package directions. Pat cream cheese mixture onto a plate; then layer meat mixture, onions, tomatoes, olives and cheddar cheese. Serve with tortilla chips and taco sauce.

Quesadillas

Beef Quesadillas

1 pound hamburger meat
3 cups of shredded cheddar or pepper jack cheese
8 large flour tortillas
1 can refried beans
Salsa
Salt & pepper

Cook hamburger meat until well done, salt and pepper to taste, drain and set aside.

In a large non-stick skillet heat a single tortilla until warm and soft, using medium heat. Remove tortilla from the skillet and spread beans on half the tortilla.

Place tortilla back into the skillet

Spoon hamburger meat and a portion of the cheese onto the beans. Fold tortilla in half and fry both sides until crisp.

Dip into salsa while eating.

Chicken Quesadillas

2 grilled chicken breast (shredded or sliced)
3 cups grated pepper jack cheese
1 cup chunky salsa
8 flour tortillas (large)
Guacamole & sour cream (for dipping)

Heat each side of a single flour tortilla in a large non-stick skillet until soft. Place chicken on half of the tortilla, cover chicken with cheese and a desired amount of salsa.

Fold the tortilla in half and fry on both sides until crisp.

Remove and enjoy!

Veggie Quesadillas

½ cup sliced mushrooms
2 diced red bell peppers
1 diced orange bell pepper
1 diced purple onion
1 cup yellow corn
2/3 cup salsa
3 cups shredded cheddar cheese
½ cup pickled jalapenos
¼ cup olive oil

Heat ¼ cup of olive oil in a medium sized skillet. Place onion, red & orange pepper and mushrooms. Heat for approximately 5 minutes then remove from heat.

Using a mixing bowl, mix fried veggies, jalapenos, corn and salsa.

Heat a single tortilla in a large non-stick skillet over medium heat, until soft. Place a portion of the veggie mixture over half the tortilla and sprinkle cheese on top.

Fold tortilla in half and cook until both sides are crispy.

Serve with pinto beans and/or Spanish rice.

So Easy Quesadillas

8 flour tortillas
1 can Rotel® tomatoes
1 pkg. shredded cheddar cheese
2 lg. cans chicken
¼ cup cooking oil

Drain tomatoes. Combine chicken, cheese, and tomatoes and heat in a sauce pan until cheese is melted (stirring occasionally). Remove from heat. Place oil into a skillet and heat, then place one tortilla onto heated oil, place chicken mixture on tortilla and spread. Place another tortilla on top. Heat both sides until tortillas are browned to your liking. Cut into triangles and eat.

Green Chili Quesadillas

2 (4 oz.) cans whole green chilies
1 8 oz block of cheddar cheese
6 flour tortillas (8 inch)
Cooking oil
Taco or picante sauce
Sour cream (opt.)

Slit chilies lengthwise; remove seeds and ribs. Cut cheese into 6 sticks. Wrap each piece of cheese in a chili. Place 1 cheese-filled chili in center of each tortilla. Fold tortillas in half over chili; fold sides inward, envelop-style. Roll and insert toothpick to secure. Fry in about 1-inch of hot oil until crisp, turning occasionally. Drain on top of paper towels. Serve immediately with taco sauce or picante salsa, and top with sour cream, if desired.

Chili Rellenos

Chili Rellenos

6 whole green chilies (2 to 3 cans)
8 oz. cheddar block
6 tablespoon flour (divided usage)
6 eggs, separated
¼ teaspoon salt
Vegetable oil (for deep-fry)
Taco or picante sauce

Slit chilies lengthwise; remove seeds and ribs. Drain on paper towels. Cut cheese into 6 strips. Stuff each chili with a strip of cheese and roll in 3 tablespoons flour. In medium mixing bowl, beat egg whites until stiff, but not dry; set aside. Combine egg yolks, 3 tablespoons flour and salt. Beat until thick and lemon-colored. Fold into egg whites. Dip chilies into egg batter, covering well. In deep-fat fryer, heat oil to 400 degrees. Fry chilies until golden brown all over. Drain on paper towels. Serve immediately with taco sauce or picante salsa.

Chili Relleno Bake

2 (4 oz.) cans green chili peppers (whole)
6 oz. Monterey Jack cheese
4 beaten eggs
1/3 cup milk
½ cup all-purpose flour
½ teaspoon baking powder
½ teaspoon salt
½ cup shredded Cheddar cheese

Preheat oven 350 degrees F

Drain chili peppers; cut lengthwise and remove the seeds. Cut the Monterey Jack cheese into strips and place inside peppers. Wrap each half pepper around strip of the Monterey Jack Cheese; place in a 10 x 6 x 2 inch baking pan. Combine milk & eggs; whip in the ½ cup of flour, baking powder & salt until smooth. Evenly pour over the peppers. Sprinkle the Cheddar cheese atop. Bake until golden, approximately 30 minutes. Makes six servings.

Burritos

Beef Burritos

1lb hamburger meat
1 can of chili (with beans)
1 small can chopped green chilies
1 ½ cups salsa (chunky style)
2 cups shredded cheddar cheese
8 flour tortillas
½ onion chopped

Cook hamburger meat and onion in a large skillet over medium heat, until meat is well done. Drain meat and stir in salsa, chili and chilies, bringing to a full boil. Reduce heat and simmer uncovered for five minutes. Place 2 to 3 tablespoons onto a flour tortilla, top with shredded cheese and roll up. If desired you can add sour cream.

Breakfast Burritos

8 eggs beaten
8-10 flour tortillas
2 cups cheddar cheese (shredded)
Cooked breakfast sausage, bacon or ham
½ cup chopped green bell pepper
½ chopped onion (optional)
Salt and pepper to taste

Scrabble eggs and heat tortillas in preheated skillet. Place a portion of each ingredient onto tortilla and roll. Great with salsa, jalapenos, chopped tomatoes, etc.

Turkey Bacon Burrito

5 eggs
¼ cup milk
½ cup salsa
6 slices turkey bacon or pork bacon
½ cup pickled jalapeno (sliced)
½ cup shredded cheddar cheese
4 to 5 flour tortillas

Place all the eggs in a small bowl and add milk then whisk. Fry bacon in skillet until crisp, once bacon is cooled, crumble it up onto a dish. Pour eggs and cheese into skillet and scramble till light and fluffy. Wrap tortillas in a damp paper towel and heat in the microwave for 1 minute. Place bacon, eggs, salsa and jalapenos onto a flour tortilla then wrap and eat.

Roxitos Burritos

8 oz. skinless & boneless chicken breast
3 teaspoon olive oil
2 garlic cloves, minced
½ small onion, chopped
15 oz. can refried beans
Tabasco
4 (10 inch) flour tortillas
1 cup shredded Monterey Jack

Salsa:
1 cup diced tomatoes
½ c diced, seeded, and peeled cucumber
¼ cup diced red onion
2 tablespoons. chopped fresh cilantro

Cut chicken into strips (about ½ inch). Combine all salsa ingredients in small bowl. Season to taste with salt. Can be prepared up to 8 hours ahead. Cover with plastic and refrigerate. Combine chicken, 2 teaspoons olive oil, and 1 clove garlic in medium bowl. Season with pepper. Place in the refrigerator for 15 minutes to 1 hour.

Heat a heavy large nonstick skillet over high heat. Add chicken mixture and sauté until the chicken is cooked through out, about 4 minutes. Transfer to plate. Heat 1 teaspoon olive oil in same skillet over medium-low heat. Add onion; cover and cook until the onion is very tender, stirring occasionally, about 8 minutes.

Stir in remaining garlic clove and sauté 1 minute. Mix in beans. Remove bean mixture from heat and season to taste with hot pepper sauce. Mix in cooked chicken.

Preheat oven 350 degrees F

Spoon ¼ of bean and chicken filling down center of 1 tortilla. Top filing with 2 tablespoons salsa. Roll up burrito. Place burrito in 9 x 13 inch baking dish, seam side down. Repeat with remaining tortillas and filling and 6 tablespoons salsa. Sprinkle cheese over burritos. Cover with foil and bake until burritos are heated through, about 15 minutes. Serve with remaining salsa.

Mexican Meat Pies

Frito Pie

2 cans chili
1 bag of Fritos
2 ½ cups grated Colby jack or cheddar cheese
1 diced yellow onion
½ head of lettuce (thinly diced)
1 yellow onion (diced)
2 to 3 diced tomatoes

Heat chili in sauce pan over medium heat stirring occasionally until boiling. In individual bowls, place a handful of Fritos, then a portion of chili, cheese, lettuce, tomato and onion. Top with sour cream if desired.

Tamale Pie

1 lb. ground beef
1 ½ cups cheddar cheese (shredded)
1 can chili with or without beans
2 heaping cup of regular Frito corn chips
1 medium onion (chopped)

Preheat oven to 350 degrees F

Brown ground beef in skillet, (salt & pepper to taste) drain and set aside. In a baking dish layer the above ingredients into two layers. Bake for 30 minutes or until hot and bubbly. Serve with tortilla chips, sour cream or salsa.

Oven Baked Frito Pie

1 can chili or 2 cups homemade chili
3 cups corn chips (Fritos)
½ cup thinly diced onion (yellow or sweet onion)
1 cup cheddar cheese (shredded)
1small can diced pickled jalapenos (optional)

Preheat oven to 350 degrees F

In a baking dish spread out 2 cups of corn chips. Sprinkle half the jalapenos, shredded cheese and diced onion over the corn chips. Pour chili over the jalapenos, cheese and onion. Sprinkle the remainder of the jalapeno, cheese, onion and Fritos.

Bake 15 to 20 minutes.

Tasty Taco Pie

1.5 lbs. ground beef
½ medium yellow onion (chopped)
1 8oz. can tomato sauce
1 pkg. taco seasoning
1 cup sour cream
1 small can sliced ripe olives
1 can crescent rolls
1 cup cheddar cheese (shredded)
Shredded lettuce & diced tomato (to top off)

Preheat oven 375 degrees F

Brown ground beef and onion in skillet and drain.
Stir in tomato sauce, seasoning mix and olives.
Separate rolls and form crust in a pie pan. (Preferably glass)
Top with sour cream & cheese
Bake for 20 to 25 minutes (crust should be golden brown)
Top with lettuce and tomato.

Nacho Pie

1 pound ground beef
½ onion (chopped)
1 can tomato sauce (8 oz)
2 tablespoons taco seasoning
1 tube crescent rolls (8 oz)
1 ½ cups crushed tortilla chips
1 container sour cream (8 oz)
1 cup pepper jack cheese (shredded)

Preheat oven 350 degree F

In skillet cook ground beef with onion. Mix in tomato sauce and taco seasoning. Bring to boil. Reduce heat and simmer for 5 minutes, uncovered. Separate the crescent dough into 8 triangles & place in a greased 9 inch pie plate. Press dough against the bottom and the sides to form a crust; seal all perforations.

Spread 1 cup tortilla chips over crust and then the meat mixture. Evenly spread sour cream over the meat mixture. Sprinkle with remaining chips & cheese. Bake 20 to 25 minutes or until crust is brown & cheese is completely melted. Let cool for 5 minutes.

Impossible Taco Pie

1 pound of ground beef
½ cup onion (chopped)
1 pkg. taco seasoning
1 can Rotel® tomatoes
1 ¼ cup milk
¾ cup of Bisquick
3 medium eggs
2 tomatoes (diced)
1 cup cheddar cheese (grated)
Sour cream

Preheat oven 400 degrees F

Grease pie plate 1 x ½ inch deep. Cook ground beef and onion, drain off excess fat. Stir in taco seasoning mix. Spread meat onto pie plate. Top with Rotel®. Beat Bisquick, milk and eggs until smooth. Approximately 1 minute. Pour mixture into plate. Bake in preheated oven for 25 minutes. Top off with the tomatoes and cheese. Inserted knife should come out clean. Place sour cream on individual servings.

Tamale Pie

1 pound of ground beef
1 cup onion (chopped)
1 cup green bell pepper (chopped)
2 cans of yellow corn (drained)
½ cup pitted ripe olives (chopped)
1 clove garlic, minced
1 Tbsp. sugar
2 to 3 teaspoons chili powder
1 ½ cup sharp cheddar cheese (grated)
1 can of tomato sauce
¾ cup yellow corn meal
2 cups water (cold)
1 tablespoon butter
½ teaspoon salt & pepper

Preheat oven 375 degrees F

Cook the ground beef, green bell pepper & onion inside a large skillet until meat is light brown and the veggies become tender. Drain the excess fat. Stir in the tomato sauce, corn, olives, garlic, sugar, chili powder, salt and pepper. Simmer until thick (20 to 25 minutes). Add cheese; stir until melted. Turn into well-greased 9 x 9 x 2 inch baking dish. Topping: Mix corn meal and ½ teaspoon salt into water. Cook, stirring until thick. Stir in butter. Spoon evenly over hot meat mixture. Bake for about 40 to 45 minutes. Serves 6.

Fajitas

Sizzling Fajitas

1 lb. sliced beef, chicken, or pork
2 cloves garlic, minced
1 teaspoon cumin
Dash of oregano
1 teaspoon salt (approximate)
2 tablespoons lemon, lime, or orange juice
2 tablespoons vinegar
1 onion (sliced)
1 green bell pepper (sliced)
Dash of hot sauce
4 flour tortillas

Slice meat of choice into 8-inch strips. Mix cumin, garlic, oregano, salt, juice, vinegar and hot sauce. Pour over meat and marinate. Heat oil in heavy pan. Stir fry meat, onion and peppers. Serve with heated tortillas, salsa, sour cream and grated cheese. Roll and eat. For a quick marinade, use Italian dressing.

Chicken Fajita Potatoes

4 large baking potatoes
1 medium red or green bell pepper, cut into strips
¼ cup chopped onion
1 tablespoon margarine or butter
1 pkg. taco seasoning mix
1 (2 oz.) can sliced black olives, drained
6 ounces cooked chicken breasts, cut into strips
½ cup (2 ounces) shredded Monterey Jack cheese
2 tablespoons diced canned green chilies
1 cup salsa
Sour cream
Guacamole

Scrub the potatoes and pat dry. Prick the skins with a fork and arrange the potatoes in a microwave-safe pie plate. Microwave, covered with waxed paper, on high for 15 to 18 minutes or until the potatoes are tender. Saute the bell pepper and onion in the margarine in a saucepan over medium heat until tender. Add the taco seasoning mix and sauté for 1 minute longer.

Remove from the heat. Add the olives, chicken, cheese and chilies and mix well. Cut a slit in each potato from end to end and squeeze to open the slit. Divide the bell pepper and onion mixture among the potatoes. Spoon ¼ cup salsa onto each potato. Microwave for 5 to 7 minutes or until heated through. Garnish the potatoes with sour cream, guacamole and additional salsa. Yield: 4 servings.

More Tex-Mex Meat Dishes

Mexican Pile On with Pecans & Coconut

1.5 lbs. ground beef
1 medium onion (chopped)
2 cups cheddar cheese (shredded)
½ head of lettuce (finely shredded)
2 tomatoes (diced)
1 cup shredded coconut
1 or ½ cup of chopped pecans
1 cup salsa (mild or hot)
1 bag of tortillas chips

Here is a delicious meal that is filling and so easy to prepare.

Cook ground beef in skillet, salt & pepper to taste then drain and place in a serving bowl. Place each ingredient into a separate bowl and line up in buffet style. For each serving, cover plate with chips first then hamburger and so on.

Peccadillo

2 tablespoons olive oil
4 boneless chicken breasts (thinly sliced)
1 medium onion (chopped)
1 garlic clove (crushed)
½ teaspoon ground cumin
½ cup pimiento stuffed olives
1 ½ cup salsa
¼ cup raisins
4 large flour tortillas

Heat olive oil in a non-stick 12 inch skillet until hot. Place sliced chicken breast into skillet and cook 4 to 7 minutes, only turn once. Once done, remove chicken from skillet and place into a bowl.
Reduce heat to medium setting, place chopped onion into skillet a cook until brown and translucent. Stir in the cumin & garlic and cook for approximately 1 minute. Stir in the remaining ingredients and heat until boiling over medium heat.
Using a damp paper towel, wrap the 4 flour tortillas and heat in the microwave for 1 minute. Spoon peccadillo onto tortilla and enjoy.

Tex-Mex Chicken Stew

1 cup of uncooked pinto beans
1 ½ lbs. boneless & skinless chicken thigh
2 tablespoons white flour
1 ½ cups chunky salsa
1 medium purple onion (chopped)
1 green bell pepper (chopped)
¼ cup sour cream
¼ cup cilantro (chopped)
3 tablespoons chopped chipotle chilies in adobo sauce
1 cup water
Salt & pepper

Combine salsa, beans, chilies, flour and water in a 6 quart slow cooker. Sprinkle salt & pepper onto chicken thighs and place them into slow cooker on top of bean mixture. Place bell pepper & onion on top of chicken.
Cover slow cooker and cook at low heat for approximately 8 hours. (Do not remove lid during cooking)
Once done, remove chicken and shred then return to stew.
Top servings with sour cream and cilantro if desired.

Tex-Mex Pork Chops

4 pork chops
1 teaspoon cooking oil
1 ½ cups chunky salsa
1 can diced green chilies
½ teaspoon ground cumin
½ cup cheddar cheese (shredded)

In a medium bowl, mix salsa, green chilies, and cumin. In a non-stick skillet brown one side of the pork chops in oil over medium heat for 2 minutes. Turn pork chops and pour mixture over the top of the pork chops, lower heat, cover and simmer for 6 minutes.

Uncover and top each pork chop with evenly portions of cheddar cheese. Cover and simmer until cheese is melted and serve.

Tortilla Pinwheels

10 lg. flour tortillas
16 oz. sour cream
1 pkg. taco season mix
10 slices ham
10 slices turkey
1 small can chopped olives
Lettuce, shredded
1 onion, chopped (opt.)
16 oz. shredded cheese

Mix taco mix with sour cream. Place approximately 2 tablespoons sour cream taco mix on tortilla (smooth over entire tortilla). Add one slice each ham and turkey. Top with approximately 1/8 cup lettuce, 1 teaspoon olives and 2 tablespoons cheese. Roll up and chill for 2 to 4 hours. Cut in 1 to 2-inch pinwheel pieces.

Tex-Mex Lasagna

1 pound of lean ground beef
1 can of refried beans (16 oz.)
2 tablespoons dried oregano
¾ tablespoon powdered garlic
2 ½ cup mild, chunky picante sauce
1 pkg. of lasagna noodles (12 ct. uncooked)
2 ½ cups water
2 cups sour cream
1 can black olives (sliced)
1 cup Monterey Jack cheese (grated)

Preheat oven 350 degrees F

Brown ground beef and drain off excess fat. All other ingredients are added uncooked. Combine beef, beans and spices. Grease bottom of a 9 x 13-inch pan. Put 4 noodles in pan. Spread half of meat mixture over noodles. Add 4 more noodles, then remaining meat. Add 4 more noodles. Mix picante sauce and water. Pour over pan ingredients. Bake for 1 ½ to 2 hours. Cover with foil for the last hour. Combine sour cream and olives. Spread over top and top with cheese. Bake an additional 5 minutes.

Mexican Hot Dish

1 lb. ground beef, browned and drained
1 onion, diced
1 can chili beans
1 can hot enchilada sauce
1 pkg. taco seasoning mix
1 cup grated cheddar cheese
1 (8 oz.) can tomato sauce
Tortilla chips

Preheat oven 350 degrees F

Combine all ingredients and bake 20 minutes. To serve, crush tortilla chips and spoon casserole over chips.

Mexican Chicken

4 whole chicken breasts
Pepper & salt (to taste)
1 can of cream of chicken soup
1 can Rotel ® tomatoes
Bay leaf
1 can cream of mushroom soup
2 onions, chopped
3 cups sharp cheddar (grated)
1 pkg. tortilla chips
Sour cream

Preheat oven 350 degrees F

Cook four (4) chicken breasts with salt, pepper, and bay leaf. Break into bit-size pieces. Mix cream of mushroom and chicken soups, 1 can Rotel ® tomatoes, and the 2 chopped onions. Layer the chicken, soup mix, and cheese. Make several layers. Bake for 45 minutes. Serve on tortilla chips and top with sour cream.

Salads

Texas Taco Salad

½ head of ice berg lettuce (finely chopped)
3 diced tomatoes
1 diced purple onion
1 ½ lb. ground beef
1 small can chopped black olives
½ cup jalapenos
2 cups shredded cheddar cheese
1 bag of tortilla chips
Salsa
Salt & pepper
Sour cream
Guacamole

Cook ground beef in large skillet until well done (salt & pepper to taste), drain and set aside. In individual serving bowls layer a portion of the lettuce, ground beef, cheese, black olives, tomatoes, onion, jalapenos and salsa. Stick tortilla chips between the bowl and the salad, all the way around. Top with sour cream and guacamole.

Cheesy Taco Salad

1.5 lbs. ground beef
1 cup chopped onion
1 cup chopped green bell pepper
2 garlic cloves (minced)
1 tablespoon cumin powder
1 pkg. taco seasoning
1 lb. Velveeta cheese
1 head of lettuce (shredded)
2 to 4 tomatoes (diced)
1 bag of Fritos

Brown ground beef and drain, add taco seasoning and cook according to the directions on the pkg. Mix the first 5 ingredients into the ground beef. Melt cheese and pour over shredded lettuce, add tomatoes and Fritos and toss lightly. Place meat mixture on top of salad and enjoy.

Mexican Corn Relish Salad

2 (16 oz.) pkgs. frozen corn, defrosted and drained
2 tomatoes (squeezed & diced)
1 can kidney beans, rinsed and drained
1 (2 ¼ oz.) can sliced ripe olives
2 green onions (chopped)
1 tablespoon of red wine vinegar
½ to ¾ teaspoon cumin
1/8 teaspoon cayenne pepper
1 teaspoon chili powder
¼ tsp seasoned salt
3 tablespoon salad oil

Combine corn, tomatoes, beans, green onions and olives. In separate bowl combine vinegar, cumin cayenne, chili powder and salt. Whisk in oil and pour over the corn salad, mixing well.

Taco Salad

1 lb. ground beef
2 medium chopped onions (divided)
1 can mild enchilada sauce
1 (15 oz.) can kidney beans
Salt and pepper
Lettuce (shredded)
Tomatoes (diced)
Taco flavored or plain tortilla chips
Shredded cheddar cheese

Brown ground beef. Add one half of chopped onion, kidney beans and enchilada sauce. Heat through. Pour over lettuce, tomatoes (if desired) and broken up tortilla chips. Top with remainder of chopped onion and shredded cheddar cheese. Add sour cream on top if desired.

Taco Frito Salad

2 cans chili beans plus sauce
1 ½ cup shredded cheddar cheese
1 ½ cup chopped onion
2 large tomatoes, chopped
1 small bottle creamy Italian dressing
1 (10 ½ oz.) bag regular Fritos
1 lb. hamburger (optional)

Mix first five ingredients together. Just before serving, add 1 (10 ½ ounce) bag regular Fritos and 1 ½ head of lettuce, shredded. Optional: Can add 1 pound browned hamburger.

Mexican Salad

1 head lettuce (shredded)
4 medium tomatoes (diced)
6 oz. cheddar cheese, cubed
1 medium onion, cut in rings
1 (5 ½ oz.) bag tortilla chips
1 can kidney beans
1 lb. ground meat
8 oz bottle Russian or French dressing

Brown the ground meat. Add 1 can kidney beans & simmer 10 minutes. Cool. Toss all ingredients lightly with dressing (all 8 ounces). Season with salt, pepper and pepper sauce to taste. Serves 8 or 10.

Steak Taco Salad

1 ½ lbs. ground round
16 oz. cottage cheese
1 (8 oz.) pkg. cream cheese, softened
1 pkg. taco seasoning
1 pkg. (2 cups) shredded cheddar cheese
1 large head lettuce (shredded)
2 tomatoes (chopped)
1 onion (chopped)
½ green pepper (chopped)
1 small can of black olives (chopped)
1 small can of green olives (chopped)
Taco sauce
Tortilla chips

Mix cottage cheese and cream cheese and spread two-thirds of it in a 9 x 13-inch pan. Brown beef, drain and add ½ pkg. Taco seasoning. Cool and spread on top of cheese. Top with remaining cheese mixture and refrigerate. Mix all vegetables and olives and shredded cheese. One hour before serving mix lettuce with vegetables and olives, etc. and spread in pan. Top with chips and sauce or serve sauce separately.

Delicious Taco Salad

1 lb. ground beef (lean)
1 pkg. taco seasoning
2 green onions (chopped)
1 green bell pepper (chopped)
2 large tomatoes (chopped)
1 (2 oz.) can sliced black olives
1 (16 oz.) pinto beans
1 ½ cups cheddar cheese (shredded)
1 large head romaine lettuce (shredded)
2 (16 oz.) packages corn chips
½ (8 oz.) bottle of Catalina salad dressing

Cook ground beef with taco seasoning according to package directions. Add green onions, green pepper, pinto beans and olives (let simmer). Toss lettuce, tomatoes, cheese, corn chips, and salad dressing place on top of meat mixture and serve. Yield 15 servings.

Soups

Mexican Cheese Soup

6 med. potatoes, peeled and diced
3 tablespoons butter
1 med. onion (chopped)
1 small can chopped green chilies
1 lg. tomato, peeled, seeded and chopped
2 ½ cups of milk or half & half
1 lb. pepper jack cheese (shredded)
Salt & pepper
Parsley or cilantro (chopped)

Place potatoes in a saucepan of salted water, bring to a boil; cover and reduce heat. Cook potatoes until tender. <u>Do not drain</u>.
Mash potatoes in saucepan, add butter and mix. Add onions, green chilies, tomatoes, milk and cheese.
Stir over medium heat until cheese is melted. Do not boil. Season to taste with salt & pepper. Add additional milk if needed to achieve desired consistency.
Serve hot, garnished with parsley or cilantro.

Texas Taco Soup

1 ½ lbs. ground beef
1 pkg. of taco seasoning
2 cans yellow corn, (do not drain)
2 (15 oz.) cans ranch-style beans (do not drain)
2 (14 ½ oz.) cans sliced tomatoes, (do not drain)
1 bag tortilla chips (crushed)
2 cups cheddar cheese (shredded)
Flour tortillas, warmed

In a large saucepan cook ground beef over medium heat until done; drain. Mix in taco seasoning, beans, tomatoes and corn. Cover pan and simmer for 15 minutes or until heated through out, stirring occasionally. In soup bowls place crushed chips on the bottom of bowl, then soup and last sprinkle shredded cheese on top. Serve with warmed flour tortillas. Yield: 8 to 10 servings (about 2 quarts).

Stewed Taco Soup

1 lb. hamburger
1 can beans (pinto)
1 can white corn
1 can green beans
1 can ranch style beans
1 can stewed tomatoes (14.5 oz.)
1 can diced tomato & green chilies (10 oz.)
1 pkg. taco seasoning mix
1 pkg. Ranch dressing mix (1 oz.)

In a large skillet brown beef and drain, add taco seasoning, cook as stated on back of package. Rinse and drain all beans and corn. In Dutch oven mix all ingredients together, bring to a boil. Reduce heat and simmer covered for 30 minutes.

Mexican Meatball Soup

1 egg, slightly beaten
½ cup chopped onion
¼ cup cornmeal
1 can green chili peppers (chopped)
1 clove garlic (minced)
¾ teaspoon salt
¼ teaspoon oregano
1/8 teaspoon pepper
1 pound ground beef
3 cups water
1 (16 oz.) can tomatoes, cut up
1 (8 oz.) can tomato sauce
1 tablespoon sugar
½ teaspoon chili powder

In large mixing bowl, combine egg, half of the chopped onion, cornmeal, half of the chili peppers, garlic, salt, oregano, pepper and ground beef. Mix together and shape into 48 meat balls. Set aside. In large saucepan or Dutch over combine water, undrained tomatoes, tomato sauce, remaining chili peppers, remaining chopped onion, sugar, and chili powder. Bring mixture to a boil, stirring well. Add meatballs and bring to boil again. Cover; reduce heat and simmer for 30 minutes. Yield: 8 servings.

Salsas

Zesty Salsa

1 chopped garlic clove
1 cup chopped tomato
1/8 cup chopped red onion
1 teaspoon chopped fresh jalapeno
1 fresh lime squeezed
¼ cup chopped cilantro
Salt & pepper to taste

In a medium sized bowl place all the above ingredients and mix together. Keep sauce in sealed container in the refrigerator, will keep up to 3 days.

Salsa

10 Roma tomatoes
1 medium white onion
5 jalapeno peppers
2 Anaheim peppers
2 habanera peppers
(Adjust peppers to taste)
1 teaspoon cilantro
1 teaspoon minced garlic
Parsley for garnish

(Note: protect hands when handling jalapenos as they can burn the skin)

Core and seed all the peppers. Dice peppers, tomatoes and onion, mix together. Add cilantro and garlic. Mix again. Garnish with parsley.

*For a hotter salsa add some jalapeno seeds.

Dips

Seven Layer Dip

1 pkg. taco seasoning
1 chopped tomato
¼ cup of mayonnaise
1 cup guacamole
1 can refried beans (16 oz)
Sour cream (8 oz)
2 cups shredded Colby jack cheese
1 can chopped black olives, drained
¼ cup chopped green onions

Spread refried beans onto a large serving dish, and then layer guacamole on top of beans. Using a medium sized bowl, stir together the mayonnaise, taco seasoning mix & sour cream, spread this over the layer of guacamole. Sprinkle shredded cheese over mayonnaise layer, and sprinkle green onions, black olives and tomato over the shredded cheese.

Fiesta Dip

1 cup miracle whip or mayonnaise
1 cup plain yogurt
4 tablespoons salt
4 tablespoons ground cumin
1/3 cup chili powder
4 tablespoons dried chives
1/3 cup minced onion
½ cup dried parsley
3 tablespoons of Fiesta Dip Mix

Combine all ingredients in a medium sized mixing bowl, until mixture is well blended. Cover and place in the refrigerator for 2 to 4 hrs.

Easy Chili Dip

2 cans refried beans
2 cups salsa
1 cup sour cream
1 pound hamburger meat
1 purple onion (chopped)
½ teaspoon chili powder
1 cup of Colby jack cheese (shredded)
1 small can chopped green chilies
Salt & pepper to taste

In skillet cook hamburger meat and onion until done, drain. Place hamburger and all other ingredients into a crock pot and cook on low heat, stirring occasionally until hot.

Mexican Dip

1 cream cheese (8oz)
1 sour cream (8oz)
1 pkg. taco seasoning
¾ cup cheddar cheese (shredded)
2 medium tomatoes (diced)
1 small can chopped black olives
1 head of lettuce (shredded)

In a medium sized bowl mix cream cheese, sour cream & taco mix refrigerate until firm. Place vegetables & cheddar cheese into pie plate or other dish and toss. Pour cream cheese mixture over veggies and serve.

Easy Nacho Cheese Dip

1 can Nacho cheese soup
1 can cheddar cheese soup
1 pt. sour cream
1 jar chunky salsa
1 bag of corn chips/tortilla chips

In saucepan heat soups and stir until well blended, (do not add water), place in serving bowl. Place sour cream and salsa in separate serving bowls. Dip chips in dip then sour cream and salsa. Enjoy!

Hardy Tex-Mex Dip

1 large can refried beans
1 lb. ground beef
1 medium onion (chopped)
8 oz. jar taco sauce
2 cups cheddar cheese (shredded)
8 oz. sour cream
½ cup chopped green onion
1 small can chopped green chilies
1 small can chopped black olives
1 bag tortilla chips

Preheat oven 400 degrees F

Brown onion & ground beef in skillet (drain). Spread refried beans on the bottom of a 9 x 13 pan. Top with ground beef and onion mixture, then taco sauce. Sprinkle with cheddar cheese.

Bake for 20 minutes or until hot and bubbly.

Top with sour cream, olives, green onions and chilies.

Chili Cheese Dip

1 lb. ground beef, browned & drained
1 can chili without beans
1 can refried beans
1 can chopped green chilies
1 can jalapeno relish
1 (2-3 lb.) box Velveeta cheese, melted

Mix all ingredients and heat. Serve hot.

Cheesy Taco Dip

1 ½ lbs. hamburger
1 pkg. taco seasoning
1 jar mild taco sauce
8 oz. cream cheese
2 tablespoons mayonnaise
3 cups Colby jack cheese (shredded)

Cook hamburger and drain grease from it. Add taco seasoning and taco sauce to hamburger and simmer for 10 to 15 minutes. Mix the cream cheese and mayonnaise together. Put cream cheese mixture in bottom of flat dish. Place hamburger mixture on top of cream cheese. Put grated cheese on top of hamburger. When ready to serve, place in microwave to melt cheese or serve cold. Serve with your favorite chips.

Hot Taco Cheese Dip

1 ½ lb. ground hamburger
½ cup onions, chopped
1 pkg. taco seasoning
1 lg. can stewed tomatoes 16 oz.
4 oz. cheddar cheese (shredded)
1 jar stuffed green olives (sliced)

Brown hamburger, onions and taco seasoning; simmer about 15 minutes. Add tomatoes and cheese. Simmer a bit more and when ready to serve add 4 more oz. of cheese and some sliced stuffed green olives for decoration. Drain excess fatty juice off top. Serve with tortilla chips or nacho flavored chips.

Mexican Dip

1 can refried beans
1 (8-oz.) container guacamole
1 cup sour cream
1 cup mayo
½ pkg. taco seasoning
½ cup green onions, chopped
1 (8-oz.) pkg. cheddar cheese (grated)
½ head lettuce, chopped
2 chopped, seeded tomatoes
½ cup chopped black olives

Mix together sour cream, mayo, taco seasoning, green onions and let set over night. On a round cake pan or serving tray, layer refried bean, topped with guacamole, then layer with the sour cream mixture. Next layer with cheese, all but about a half cup. Then put on layer of lettuce, then a layer of the tomatoes. Sprinkle with the remaining cheese for color and top with the black olives. Serve with your favorite chips.

Texas Caviar

2 cans black-eyed peas, drained
1 can hominy, drained
½ cup chopped cilantro
1 green pepper, chopped
1 jalapeno pepper, chopped fine
2 med. cloves garlic, chopped
1 bunch green onions, chopped
½ cup red onion, chopped
2 lg. tomatoes, chopped
1 (8-oz.) bottle Italian dressing

Mix all ingredients together and marinate at least 2 hours or overnight. Serve with tortilla chips.

Easy Taco Dip

1 lb. hamburger
1 (16 oz.) pkg. Velveeta mild Mexican cheese spread
1 can Rotel® tomatoes with green chilies, drained

Brown and drain hamburger. Mix in cheese spread and tomatoes until cheese is melted. Serve with tortilla chips.

Party Taco Dip

1 (8 oz.) pkg. cream cheese
1 pkg. original Hidden Valley dressing mix
1 sm. ctn. sour cream
1 jar taco sauce
Lettuce, shredded
Green pepper, chopped
Onion, chopped
1 can chopped black olives (small)
1 large tomato, chopped
Cheddar cheese, shredded
Tortilla chips

Mix cream cheese, dressing mix and sour cream. Put on bottom of large plate. Cover with ½ jar of taco sauce. Cover the taco sauce with layers of lettuce, green pepper, onion, ripe olives and tomato. Top with the rest of the taco sauce and cheddar cheese. Use tortilla chips to dip with.

Mexican Meat Dip

1 ½ lb ground beef
½ cup chopped onion
1 (16 oz.) can refried beans, divided
1 (4 oz.) can diced green chilies, drained & divided
1 (24 oz.) jar salsa, divided
2 cups cheddar cheese (grated)
¼ cup chopped black olives
Sour cream
Tortilla chips

Preheat oven 350 degrees F

Brown beef and onion inside a large skillet; drain. Place half of beans into a 9 x 13-inch baking dish. Layer with half of the cooked ground beef, salsa, chilies and cheese. Repeat layering with the remaining beans, beef, salsa, chilies and cheese. Bake for 30 minutes until cheese is completely melted and mixture is hot. Top with olives and serve with sour cream and tortilla chips.

Baked Nacho Dip

2 cans refried beans, 1 lb. size
1 lg. onion, chopped and sautéed
1 (4 oz.) can chopped green chilies, drained
1 bottle mild taco sauce, 11 oz. size
8 oz. shredded cheddar cheese
8 oz. shredded mozzarella cheese

Layer ingredients in order listed in a 9 x 1-inch pan. Bake at 325 degrees F for 25 minutes. Serve hot, in pan, dipping into it with tortilla chips, crackers, etc. An easy snack for a party.

Chili Dip

1 (8 oz.) brick cream cheese
1 (15-oz.) can of chili, no beans
2 cups mozzarella cheese (shredded)

Heat together until cream cheese melts. Spread into a 9-ich pie plate. Top with layer of mozzarella cheese. Heat in a microwave or oven until cheese melts. Serve with tortilla chips.

Layered Taco Dip

2 pkgs. cream cheese (8 oz)
1 pint sour cream
1 pkg. taco seasoning
1 small head of lettuce
1 bag tortilla chips

Mix all together until well blended. Chop small head of lettuce in small pieces.

1 (14-16 oz.) can sliced black olives
½ lb. cheddar cheese (shredded)
3 tomatoes (chopped)

Spread cheese mixture on large plate. Top with layers of lettuce, chopped tomatoes, ripe olives and grated cheese. Scoop up with tortilla chips.

Nacho Cheese Dip

1 lb. breakfast sausage
1 (11 oz.) can Nacho cheese soup
1 (11 oz.) can cheddar cheese soup
1 pint sour cream
1 jar salsa
1 can green chilies (chopped)

Crumble sausage in skillet and cook until done, then drain. Heat cheese soups together and add green chilies do not dilute. Stir sausage into soup. Serve with tortilla or corn chips and bowls of sour cream and salsa.

Nacho Dip

1 large can refried beans
1 lb. ground beef
1 medium onion, chopped
8 oz. jar taco sauce
2 cups grated cheddar cheese
8 oz. sour cream
½ cup chopped green onion
1 small can chopped green chilies
1 small can chopped ripe olives
1 bag tortilla chips

Brown beef and chopped onion then drain off excess fat. Spread beans in bottom of a 9 x 13-inch pan. Top with beef and onion mixture. Spread taco sauce over that. Sprinkle with cheese. Bake in 400 degree oven about 20 minutes, until cheese melts and bubbles. Top with sour cream. Sprinkle with green onion, olives and chilies. Serve as dip with tortilla chips.

Mexican Dip

1 (8 oz.) cream cheese
1 (8 oz.) sour cream
1 pkg. taco seasoning
¼ lb. shredded cheddar cheese
2 medium tomatoes (chopped)
1 can chopped olives- small
1 head shredded lettuce

Mix cream cheese, sour cream and taco mix together and let firm in refrigerator. Use pie plate or other dish and top the vegetables with the cheddar cheese and the mix of cream cheese, sour cream and taco mix. Serve with tortilla chips.

Jalapeno Corn Dip

2 (11 oz.) cans Mexicorn
1 (8 oz.) jar mayonnaise
1 (8 oz.) container of sour cream
1 (4 oz.) can chopped green chilies
2 cups (8 oz.) shredded Cheddar cheese
2 chopped jalapeno peppers
1 bunch green onions, chopped
Pinch of sugar

Combine the Mexicorn, mayonnaise, sour cream, green chilies, cheddar cheese, jalapeno peppers, green onions and sugar in a bowl and mix well. Chill, covered, in the refrigerator for 2 hours. Serve with corn or tortilla chips. Yield 25 to 30 servings.

Guacamole

Tasty Guacamole Dip

1 medium sized tomato (peeled)
2 ripe avocados
4 tablespoon minced canned chili peppers
½ cup onion (chopped)
1½ tablespoon white vinegar
Salt & pepper to taste

Smash tomato and avocado together in a medium sized bowl until well blended. Add the remainder of the ingredients. Mix well & refrigerate.

Holy Guacamole

3 ripe avocados, peeled and seeded
¼ cup chopped green onion tops
2 tablespoons fresh lemon juice
3-4 cloves garlic, pressed
1 diced tomato
1 jalapeno pepper seeded & finely chopped (to taste)
½ cup cilantro (chopped)
Salt (to taste)
Chili powder (to taste)

In medium bowl, roughly mash avocado with a fork or wire whisk. Stir in remaining ingredients. Let sit 15 minutes or longer. Serve with tortilla chips.

Breads

Texas Cornbread

1 ¼ cups plain yellow corn meal
2 eggs
1 cup buttermilk
½ cup oil
1 teaspoon salt
3 teaspoons baking powder
1 can yellow cream-style corn
1 tablespoon chopped onion
1 jar banana peppers (opt.)
1 cup grated sharp cheddar cheese

Preheat oven 375 degrees F

Mix all ingredients, except cheese in large bowl. Grease 13 x 9-inch dish and put in half of batter, then cheese and remaining batter. Bake for 45 minutes.

Mexican Cornbread

½ lb. cheddar cheese (grated)
1 lg. onion, chopped
2 cans chopped green chilies (small)
1 lb. lean hamburger
1 ½ cups yellow cornmeal
¾ teaspoon baking soda
1 ½ Tablespoon salt
3 eggs
½ cup salad oil
1 can creamed corn
1 ½ cups milk

Grease a large skillet and place in a 350 degrees oven. Brown and drain the hamburger; set aside. Mix cornmeal, soda, salt, eggs, oil, milk and corn. Remove skillet from oven. Pour half of mixture into skillet. Layer the following into skillet: cheese, onion, chilies and hamburger. Cover with second half of mixture. Bake 1 hour.

Desserts

Cinnamon Apple Enchiladas

1 can apple pie filling
1 teaspoon ground cinnamon
½ cup sugar
½ cup brown sugar
1/3 cup butter or margarine
6 flour tortillas (8 inch)
½ cup water

Preheat oven to 350 degrees F

Place a spoonful of fruit onto each tortilla and sprinkle cinnamon on top. Roll up fruit filled tortillas and place seam side down into an 8 x 8 greased baking dish. In sauce pan heat butter, brown sugar, sugar and water and bring to a boil. Reduce the heat & simmer while stirring continuously for 3 minutes. Pour sauce over rolled tortillas and sprinkle cinnamon on top. Bake for 20 minutes.

Sweet Banana Bake

4 tablespoons of honey
6 bananas
2 tablespoons of melted margarine or butter
2 tablespoons of fresh squeezed lemon juice
½ cup of chopped pecans
Chocolate syrup (optional)

Preheat oven to 325 degree F

After peeling the bananas cut each one into 3 pieces. Place the cut bananas into a shallow baking pan.

Mix lemon juice, honey and butter, then spoon mixture over the bananas.

Bake for approximately 15 minutes, turning bananas occasionally.

Once cooked, drizzle bananas with chocolate syrup, and sprinkle with pecans.

Serve hot.

Mexican Fiesta Pie

6 tablespoon butter, melted
3 tablespoon sugar
1 ¼ cups pretzels, finely ground
1 qt. vanilla ice cream, softened
½ (10 oz.) can frozen margarita concentrate, thawed
Lime twists

Preheat oven 350 degrees F

Combine butter, sugar and pretzels; pat into 9 inch glass pie plate, reserving 2 tablespoons for topping. Bake 10 minutes. Cool. Blend ice cream and 5 oz. of margarita concentrate until thoroughly combined. (Save remaining for another use, or make 2 pies). Spoon into crust. Sprinkle with remaining crumbs. Freeze. Garnish with lime slices.

Miscellaneous

Baked Jalapeno Poppers

4 fresh jalapenos
2 oz. cream cheese at room temperature
2 tablespoons of minced onion
1 tablespoon of spice mix (chili powder, cumin, paprika & black pepper)
Cornmeal
1 egg white & 1 whole egg

Preheat oven 350 degrees F

In a small bowl mix minced onion, cream cheese & spices.

*Protect hands by wearing gloves when handling peppers.

Cut off pepper stems and cut peppers lengthwise. Remove seeds & membrane. Fill each half with cream cheese mixture.

Place eggs into bowl and whip. Place a portion of cornmeal into another bowl. Dip peppers into egg & then into cornmeal.

Cover cooking sheet with oil & place filled peppers on it.

Bake for approximately 20 to 30 minutes. Peppers will be brown & crispy when done

Mexican Quick Steppers

8 oz. sharp cheddar cheese
8 oz. Monterey Jack cheese
1 small can whole green chilies
1 egg
1 small can (4 oz.) evaporated milk
Couple shakes Tabasco
1 teaspoon Worcestershire sauce
½ teaspoon salt
¼ teaspoon pepper

Preheat oven 350 degrees F

Grate all cheese and set aside. Open and drain the green chilies. Cut green chilies into strips and scatter evenly over the bottom of an ungreased 8 x 8 inch cake pan. Sprinkle all the cheese over the chilies. In small bowl beat the egg, milk and seasonings and blend together. Drizzle over cheese mixture. There will not be a great deal of liquid – but don't worry – it will all blend in when it's done.

Bake for 45 minutes or until its set like custard. Slice into small pieces and serve hot. Warning: this may be too hot for some, so go easy on the Tabasco, and rinse and drain the chilies in cold water before using if you like it less hot.

My Mexican Deviled Eggs

8 hard boiled eggs
½ cup cheddar cheese (shredded)
¼ cup mayonnaise
¼ cup salsa
1 tablespoon sour cream
2 tablespoons green onions (chopped)
Salt to taste

Halve the egg lengthwise; remove the yolks to a small bowl. Arrange the whites, hollow side up, on a plate. Add the mayonnaise, cheese, salsa, green onions, sour cream and salt to the yolks and mash well. Fill the whites evenly with the yolk mixture. Serve immediately or chill until ready to serve. Yield: 16 servings.

Photo credits:
Cover photo by KirbyIng/Photos.com
Back cover photo by Sarah Bossert/Photos.com

TEX-MEX RECIPES

CPSIA information can be obtained
at www.ICGtesting.com
Printed in the USA
FSOW03n1150070917
38471FS